the Catalogue of Hugs

by Joshua David Stein
and Augustus Heeren Stein
art by Elizabeth Lilly

RISE

NEW YORK

For: _____

With Hugs From: _____

RISE × Penguin Workshop

An imprint of Penguin Random House LLC, New York

First published in the United States of America by Rise × Penguin Workshop,
an imprint of Penguin Random House LLC, New York, 2022

Text copyright © 2022 by Joshua David Stein
Illustrations copyright © 2022 by Elizabeth Lilly

Visit us online at penguinrandomhouse.com.

Library of Congress Cataloging-in-Publication Data is available.

Manufactured in China

ISBN 9780593521793   10 9 8 7 6 5 4 3 2 1 HH

The text is set in ITC Veljovic Std.
The art was created digitally using Photoshop on a Wacom Cintiq drawing tablet.

Edited by Cecily Kaiser
Designed by Maria Elias

To everyone (and anyone)
who needs a hug.
—JDS & AHS

To Elena, who sends me
hugs with every email.
Xoxo forever.
—EL

the

Classic

the
Sloth

the

Koala

the

Backpack

the

Frontpack

the
Hat

the
Tower

the
Blindfold

the

Flying Squirrel

the

Upside Down

the

Necklace

the

T-Shirt

the

Leg Hug

the

Partial Leg Hug

the

Tantrum Hug

the

Sleep Hug

the

Tuck In

the
Otter

the
Head Hold

the

Walking Hug

the

Rolling Hug

the

Work from Home Hug

the

Long-Distance Hug

the

Hug for One

the
Family Hug

Want more hugs?
Try these:

the
Armadillo

the
Bus Stop

the
Toaster

the
Kitten Hug

the
Tuba

the
Puppy Hug

the
Hot Cocoa

the
Nautilus

the
Pillowcase

the
Pile

the

Pill Bug

the

Kangaroo

the

Statue

the

Spaghetti
and Meatballs

the

Fishy Hug

the

Paratha

the

Parachute

the

Ballet Hug

the

Boogie Down

the

Mind Hug

the

Tree Hug

the

Opossum